# Ten P[oems]
# by The R[omantics]

ex libris

Candlestick Press

Published by:
Candlestick Press,
DiVersity House, 72 Nottingham Road,
Arnold, Nottingham NG5 6LF
www.candlestickpress.co.uk

Design, typesetting, print and production by DiVersity Creative
Marketing Solutions Ltd., www.diversity-nottm.co.uk

Cover Illustration: © Peter Reddick
Introduction: © Catherine Kay, 2011

ISBN 978 1 907598 05 0

The publisher thanks the Estate of Peter Reddick for permission to
reproduce his illustration to the poetry of William Wordsworth on the cover.

Thanks are also due to Catherine Kay of The Wordsworth Trust
for her Introduction.

# Introduction

The poetry of what we now call the Romantic period is as rich and varied as the time itself, covering as it does the end of one century (the eighteenth) and the birth of another. Although there were bonds of friendship and ideas between some of the poets, none considered themselves 'Romantic' and, in fact, might be surprised to learn that more than 200 years later their poems sit side by side in many anthologies.

What much of the poetry of the Romantic period shares is a passionate belief in the transforming power of the imagination and a related faith in the human spirit. For Wordsworth and Coleridge it is Nature that so often provides the key to unlocking that power and restoring the human spirit in times of need; whereas Shelley and Keats (especially in the poems in this selection) use objects from the physical world to transport them to worlds of the imagination.

All the writers too explore the world of feeling. The period begins with pensive emotion in which dreamscapes feature heavily, but as the period progresses poets lose their fear of probing their own emotional responses and development. Memory becomes an important theme, not just for understanding past emotion, but also for revealing a possible future – Coleridge uses his own past and present to imagine a future for his baby son in 'Frost at Midnight'. The later Romantics often explore extremes of emotion and our fascination with the dark side of human nature – hence the Byronic hero.

The poems in this selection are an introduction to the ideas and themes of Romantic poetry, and also to its beauty and music.


*Catherine Kay,*
*Education Officer, The Wordsworth Trust*

# Contents

# She walks in Beauty

She walks in beauty, like the night
Of cloudless climes and starry skies;
And all that's best of dark and bright
Meet in her aspect and her eyes:
Thus mellow'd to that tender light
Which heaven to gaudy day denies.

One shade the more, one ray the less,
Had half impair'd the nameless grace
Which waves in every raven tress,
Or softly lightens o'er her face;
Where thoughts serenely sweet express
How pure, how dear their dwelling-place.

And on that cheek, and o'er that brow,
So soft, so calm, yet eloquent,
The smiles that win, the tints that glow,
But tell of days in goodness spent,
A mind at peace with all below,
A heart whose love is innocent.

*George Gordon (Lord) Byron (1788 - 1824)*

# The Solitary Reaper

Behold her, single in the field,
Yon solitary Highland lass,
Reaping and singing by herself;
Stop here, or gently pass.
Alone she cuts and binds the grain,
And sings a melancholy strain;
O listen! for the vale profound
Is overflowing with the sound.

No nightingale did ever chaunt
More welcome notes to weary bands
Of travellers in some shady haunt,
Among Arabian sands:
A voice so thrilling ne'er was heard
In spring-time from the cuckoo-bird,
Breaking the silence of the seas
Among the farthest Hebrides.

Will no one tell me what she sings? –
Perhaps the plaintive numbers flow
For old, unhappy, far-off things,
And battles long ago:
Or is it some more humble lay,
Familiar matter of today?
Some natural sorrow, loss or pain,
That has been and may be again?

Whate'er the theme, the maiden sang
As if her song could have no ending;
I saw her singing at her work,
And o'er the sickle bending; –
I listened, motionless and still;
And, as I mounted up the hill,
The music in my heart I bore,
Long after it was heard no more.

*William Wordsworth (1770 - 1850)*

## A Poison Tree

I was angry with my friend:
I told my wrath, my wrath did end.
I was angry with my foe:
I told it not, my wrath did grow.

And I water'd it in fears,
Night and morning with my tears;
And I sunned it with smiles,
And with soft deceitful wiles.

And it grew both day and night,
Till it bore an apple bright;
And my foe beheld it shine,
And he knew that it was mine,

And into my garden stole
When the night had veil'd the pole:
In the morning glad I see
My foe outstretch'd beneath the tree.


*William Blake (1757 - 1827)*

# Frost at Midnight

The Frost performs its secret ministry,
Unhelped by any wind. The owlet's cry
Came loud – and hark, again! loud as before.
The inmates of my cottage, all at rest,
Have left me to that solitude, which suits
Abstruser musings: save that at my side
My cradled infant slumbers peacefully.
'Tis calm indeed! so calm, that it disturbs
And vexes meditation with its strange
And extreme silentness. Sea, hill, and wood,
This populous village! Sea, and hill, and wood,
With all the numberless goings-on of life,
Inaudible as dreams! the thin blue flame
Lies on my low-burnt fire, and quivers not;
Only that film*, which fluttered on the grate,
Still flutters there, the sole unquiet thing.
Methinks, its motion in this hush of nature
Gives it dim sympathies with me who live,
Making it a companionable form,
Whose puny flaps and freaks the idling Spirit
By its own moods interprets, every where
Echo or mirror seeking of itself,
And makes a toy of Thought.

              But O! how oft,
How oft, at school, with most believing mind,
Presageful, have I gazed upon the bars,
To watch that fluttering stranger! and as oft
With unclosed lids, already had I dreamt
Of my sweet birth-place, and the old church-tower,
Whose bells, the poor man's only music, rang
From morn to evening, all the hot Fair-day,
So sweetly, that they stirred and haunted me
With a wild pleasure, falling on mine ear

Most like articulate sounds of things to come!
So gazed I, till the soothing things, I dreamt,
Lulled me to sleep, and sleep prolonged my dreams!
And so I brooded all the following morn,
Awed by the stern preceptor's face, mine eye
Fixed with mock study on my swimming book:
Save if the door half opened, and I snatched
A hasty glance, and still my heart leaped up,
For still I hoped to see the stranger's face,
Townsman, or aunt, or sister more beloved,
My play-mate when we both were clothed alike!

   Dear Babe, that sleepest cradled by my side,
Whose gentle breathings, heard in this deep calm,
Fill up the interspersèd vacancies
And momentary pauses of the thought!
My babe so beautiful! it thrills my heart
With tender gladness, thus to look at thee,
And think that thou shalt learn far other lore,
And in far other scenes! For I was reared
In the great city, pent 'mid cloisters dim,
And saw nought lovely but the sky and stars.
But *thou*, my babe! shalt wander like a breeze
By lakes and sandy shores, beneath the crags
Of ancient mountain, and beneath the clouds,
Which image in their bulk both lakes and shores
And mountain crags: so shalt thou see and hear
The lovely shapes and sounds intelligible
Of that eternal language, which thy God
Utters, who from eternity doth teach
Himself in all, and all things in himself.
Great universal Teacher! he shall mould
Thy spirit, and by giving make it ask.

Therefore all seasons shall be sweet to thee,
Whether the summer clothe the general earth
With greenness, or the redbreast sit and sing
Betwixt the tufts of snow on the bare branch
Of mossy apple-tree, while the nigh thatch
Smokes in the sun-thaw; whether the eave-drops fall
Heard only in the trances of the blast,
Or if the secret ministry of frost
Shall hang them up in silent icicles,
Quietly shining to the quiet Moon.

*Samuel Taylor Coleridge (1772 - 1834)*

\*Coleridge noted: "In all parts of the kingdom these films are called strangers and supposed to portend the arrival of some absent friend."

**To Melancholy**
*Written on the banks of the Arun, October 1785*

When latest autumn spreads her evening veil,
And the grey mists from these dim waves arise,
I love to listen to the hollow sighs
Through the half-leafless wood that breathes the gale;
For at such hours the shadowy phantom pale
Oft seems to fleet before the poet's eyes –
Strange sounds are heard, and mournful melodies
As of night-wanderers who their woes bewail!
Here by his native stream at such an hour
Pity's own Otway I methinks could meet,
And hear his deep sighs swell the saddened wind.
Oh Melancholy, such thy magic power
That to the soul these dreams are often sweet,
And soothe the pensive visionary mind!


*Charlotte Smith (1749 - 1806)*

## Ode on a Grecian Urn

Thou still unravish'd bride of quietness,
Thou foster-child of silence and slow time,
Sylvan historian, who canst thus express
A flowery tale more sweetly than our rhyme:
What leaf-fring'd legend haunts about thy shape
Of deities or mortals, or of both,
In Tempe or the dales of Arcady?
What men or gods are these? What maidens loth?
What mad pursuit? What struggle to escape?
What pipes and timbrels? What wild ecstasy?

Heard melodies are sweet, but those unheard
Are sweeter; therefore, ye soft pipes, play on;
Not to the sensual ear, but, more endear'd,
Pipe to the spirit ditties of no tone:
Fair youth, beneath the trees, thou canst not leave
Thy song, nor ever can those trees be bare;
Bold Lover, never, never canst thou kiss,
Though winning near the goal – yet, do not grieve;
She cannot fade, though thou hast not thy bliss,
For ever wilt thou love, and she be fair!

Ah, happy, happy boughs! that cannot shed
Your leaves, nor ever bid the Spring adieu;
And, happy melodist, unwearièd,
For ever piping songs for ever new;
More happy love! more happy, happy love!
For ever warm and still to be enjoy'd,
For ever panting, and for ever young;
All breathing human passion far above,
That leaves a heart high-sorrowful and cloy'd,
A burning forehead, and a parching tongue.

Who are these coming to the sacrifice?
To what green altar, O mysterious priest,
Lead'st thou that heifer lowing at the skies,
And all her silken flanks with garlands drest?
What little town by river or sea shore,
Or mountain-built with peaceful citadel,
Is emptied of its folk, this pious morn?
And, little town, thy streets for evermore
Will silent be; and not a soul to tell
Why thou art desolate, can e'er return.

O Attic shape! fair attitude! with brede
Of marble men and maidens overwrought,
With forest branches and the trodden weed;
Thou, silent form, dost tease us out of thought
As doth eternity: Cold Pastoral!
When old age shall this generation waste,
Thou shalt remain, in midst of other woe
Than ours, a friend to man, to whom thou say'st,
'Beauty is truth, truth beauty, – that is all
Ye know on earth, and all ye need to know'.


*John Keats (1795 - 1821)*

# Casabianca

The boy stood on the burning deck
Whence all but he had fled;
The flame that lit the battle's wreck
Shone round him o'er the dead.

Yet beautiful and bright he stood,
As born to rule the storm;
A creature of heroic blood,
A proud, though child-like form.

The flames rolled on – he would not go
Without his father's word;
That father, faint in death below,
His voice no longer heard.

He called aloud – 'say, Father, say
If yet my task is done?'
He knew not that the chieftain lay
Unconscious of his son.

'Speak, Father!' once again he cried,
'If I may yet be gone!'
And but the booming shots replied,
And fast the flames rolled on.

Upon his brow he felt their breath,
And in his waving hair,
And looked from that lone post of death
In still yet brave despair.

And shouted but once more aloud,
'My Father! must I stay?'
While o'er him fast, through sail and shroud,
The wreathing fires made way.

They wrapt the ship in splendour wild,
They caught the flag on high,
And streamed above the gallant child,
Like banners in the sky.

There came a burst of thunder sound –
The boy – oh! where was he?
Ask of the winds that far around
With fragments strewed the sea! –

With mast, and helm, and pennon fair,
That well had borne their part –
But the noblest thing which perished there
Was that young, faithful heart.


*Felicia Hemans (1793 - 1835)*

# I wandered lonely as a cloud

I wandered lonely as a cloud
That floats on high o'er vales and hills,
When all at once I saw a crowd,
A host, of golden daffodils;
Beside the lake, beneath the trees,
Fluttering and dancing in the breeze.

Continuous as the stars that shine
And twinkle on the milky way,
They stretched in never-ending line
Along the margin of a bay:
Ten thousand saw I at a glance,
Tossing their heads in sprightly dance.

The waves beside them danced; but they
Out-did the sparkling waves in glee:
A poet could not but be gay,
In such a jocund company:
I gazed – and gazed – but little thought
What wealth the show to me had brought:

For oft, when on my couch I lie
In vacant or in pensive mood,
They flash upon that inward eye
Which is the bliss of solitude;
And then my heart with pleasure fills
And dances with the daffodils.


*William Wordsworth (1770 - 1850)*

### *From* Grasmere – a Fragment

Peaceful our valley, fair and green;
And beautiful the cottages,
Each in its nook, its sheltered hold,
Or underneath its tuft of trees.

Many and beautiful they are;
But there is one that I love best.
A lowly roof in truth it is,
A brother of the rest.

Yet when I sit on rock or hill
Down-looking on the valley fair,
That cottage with its grove of trees
Summons my heart; it settles there.

Others there are whose small domain
Of fertile fields with hedgerows green
Might more seduce the traveler's mind
To wish that there his home had been.

Such wish be his! I blame him not;
My fancies they, perchance, are wild:
I love that house because it is
The very mountain's child.


*Dorothy Wordsworth (1771 - 1855)*

## Ozymandias

I met a traveller from an antique land
Who said: Two vast and trunkless legs of stone
Stand in the desert. Near them, on the sand,
Half sunk, a shattered visage lies, whose frown,
And wrinkled lip, and sneer of cold command,
Tell that its sculptor well those passions read
Which yet survive, stamped on these lifeless things,
The hand that mocked them, and the heart that fed:
And on the pedestal these words appear:
'My name is Ozymandias, king of kings:
Look on my works, ye Mighty, and despair!'
Nothing beside remains. Round the decay
Of that colossal wreck, boundless and bare
The lone and level sands stretch far away.


*Percy Bysshe Shelley (1792 - 1822)*